Y0-EHY-412

THE SLEEPING BEAUTY

THE·SLEEPINC
BEAUTY

TOLD·BY·C·S·EVANS
AND·ILLUSTRATED·BY
ARTHUR·RACKHAM

Exeter Books

NEW YORK

Original edition first published in Great Britain in 1920 by
William Heinemann Ltd

This edition first published in 1972

Published in USA 1987 by Exeter Books.
Distributed by Bookthrift Marketing, Inc.
Exeter is a trademark of Bookthrift Marketing, Inc.
Bookthrift is a registered trademark of Bookthrift
Marketing, Inc., New York, New York.

By arrangement with Octopus Books Limited

ISBN 0-671-08748-7

Printed in Hong Kong

BRIAR·ROSE

ONCE·UPON·A·TIME

THE
SLEEPING BEAUTY

CHAPTER I

ONCE upon a time there were a King and a Queen who were very unhappy because they had no children. Everything else that the heart could wish for was theirs. They were rich; they lived in a wonderful palace full of the costliest treasures; their kingdom was at peace, and their people were prosperous.

10　Yet none of these things contented them, because they wanted a little child of their own to love and to care for, and though they had been married several years, no child had come to them.

Every day the King would look at the Queen and say : " Ah, if we only had a little child," and the Queen would look at the King and sigh, and they were both very miserable about it. Then they would put on their golden crowns

and sit side by side on their thrones, while lords and ladies
and ambassadors from other lands came to pay them homage,
and they had to smile with their lips for the sake of polite-
ness, but there was no joy in their hearts.   And that is one
of the greatest disadvantages of being a King or a Queen,
that one has always to hide one's feelings.

Now it happened one day that the Queen went to her
bath, and having dismissed her ladies, she descended the

marble steps into the water and began idly to play with some wild rose-petals which had fallen into the water. All of a sudden she heard a croaking voice that said : " O Queen, be cheerful, for the dearest wish of your heart will be granted you."

"Who is that ? " cried the Queen, a little frightened, for she could see nobody.

"Look behind you," croaked the voice, "and do not be afraid, for I come only to bear you good tidings."

So the Queen looked behind her, and there was a great frog who looked at her with its big round eyes.

Now the Queen was afraid of frogs, because they are cold and clammy, but she was very polite by nature as well as breeding, so she did not show her dislike, though she could not help shrinking back a little.

"And do you tell me, Master Frog," said she, "that I shall have the wish of my heart, and do you know what that wish may be ? "

"It is to have a little small child of your own," said the Frog ; and the Queen nodded.

"Very well," the Frog went on, "do you see the green leaves of that almond tree on the branch by the window ? "

"I do," replied the Queen wonderingly.

"Those green leaves will fade," said the Frog, "and the winter winds will blow them away. Then the branch will be bare, but in spring-time, before the leaves come again, it will be covered with pink blossom, and that blossom you shall show to a baby lying at your breast."

The Queen gave a cry of joy. A ray of sunlight came through the trees, dazzling her eyes so that she had to close

them for a moment.　When she opened them again the frog had gone, and nothing was to be seen but the dainty rose-petals floating on the surface of the water.

CHAPTER II

THOSE were wonderful tidings to be spoken by a frog who came no one knew whence and went no one knew whither. But the Queen believed that the prophecy would prove true, and she was right, for when the Spring time came again and the almond blossom was pink upon the bough, she gave birth to a little daughter who was so beautiful that nobody had ever seen her like.

Now what joy there was in the hearts of everybody in the palace! The King was so excited that he went into council in his dressing-gown instead of his royal robe, and he did not care a bit when his courtiers smiled. There was coming and going in all the halls and corridors. Couriers on swift horses were sent out to bear the glad news to the most distant parts of the kingdom. All the bells in the churches were rung; flags were put out in the houses and streamers were hung across the roadways. Then the cannons were fired, bang, bang, bang, to tell the people that everybody was to have a holiday, so that all, from the highest to the lowest, might rejoice in their Queen's happiness.

"Never was there such a beautiful child," said the King, looking down at his little daughter as she lay in her mother's arms. He wanted very much to nurse her, but this could not be allowed, because men are so clumsy with babies.

"What shall her name be?" said the King. And he suggested all the grandest names he could call to mind, for he thought that such a wonderful child must certainly have a name to suit. But the Queen would have none of them.

"She shall be called Briar-Rose," said the Queen; and so it was arranged.

A few weeks later the christening took place. That was a splendid ceremony to be sure, for all the lords and

ladies of the kingdom were present in their richest dresses, together with princes and ambassadors from distant countries. The little Princess was as good as gold all the time. She did not cry once, but opened her big blue eyes and smiled at the glittering company as though she understood everything that was going on.

Outside the cathedral the

roads were crowded with people waiting to see the guests come and go. The carriages extended for nearly a mile, and as they drove away, headed by the royal coach, in which the Queen sat with the Princess Briar-Rose in her arms, the spectators took off their hats and shouted and cheered. Some of the little boys perched themselves on the branches of trees and the lamp-posts in order to get a better view, and I have been told that there was one poor woman who saw nothing at all, because her boy tried to climb up to an inn sign, where he dangled in such a dangerous position that his poor old mother had to stand with her back to the procession, holding on to his legs in a terrible state of anxiety lest he should fall.

At the palace, a magnificent feast had been prepared.

Now it was the custom in those days, when a King's child was christened, for all the fairies in the country to be invited to the christening feast. Each fairy was bound to bring a gift, so of course it stood to reason that the royal child would have everything that the heart could possibly desire.

There were thirteen fairies in the King's realm, but one of them lived in a lonely place on the outskirts of the kingdom. There, for the last fifty years, she had shut herself up in a ruined tower with only a black cat to keep her company, and as she kept herself to herself, everybody had forgotten her very existence. The result was that she was not invited to the christening feast, and though she had nobody but herself to blame for this, she was very angry about it. The truth of the matter is that she was always a

miserable, sour creature, with no love or kindness in her heart, and nobody missed her because she had never given anybody any reason to care for her.

Well, the guests assembled in the banqueting hall of the palace and the feast began.

CHAPTER III

THE King and the Queen sat on a dais at the end of the banqueting hall, and above them in a little gallery there was a band of fiddlers and flute-players. On either side of the royal pair sat the twelve fairy godmothers, six on the right hand and six on the left. In front of each fairy was a golden plate and a golden casket made to hold her knife, fork and spoon. These caskets were beautifully carved and engraved, and each one was of a different shape. One was in the form of a ship, another of a shell, a third in the form of a castle with turrets, and so on ; nothing more beautiful could be imagined, for they had all been specially made for the occasion by the cleverest goldsmiths in the kingdom, and they were the King's presents to the fairy godmothers. He felt very proud when the fairies spoke admiringly of these caskets and said that they would be pleased to accept them.

Below the dais were six long tables for the guests, and there was only just room between the tables for the servants to pass, so you may judge how crowded the room was. Such a glittering of silks, such a flashing of jewels, such a dazzle and splendour had never been seen since the time of the King's coronation, and all the guests were laughing and talking merrily. The court painter was there, of course, to make a picture of the gorgeous scene, and was kept so busy sketching on his tablets that he had no time to get any food, though probably he had a good meal afterwards.

And the nice things there were to eat ! There were :

Force-meat balls flavoured with rare spices from the East ;

Sardines from Sardinia ;

Tunny fish from the Mediterranean and Sturgeon
    from Russia ;
Steaming boars' heads with lemons in their mouths ;
Turkeys, peacocks and swans ;
Ortolans ;
Wonderful roasts and delicious stews ;
Roe deer and Bears' hams ;

Sweets in all sorts of curious shapes, as, for instance, cakes like castles with little men made of sweet-stuff for sentries on the battlements, each complete in gilded armour and with a halberd over his shoulder. (A rare sight !) And eagles carved of ice hovering over silver dishes filled with apricots.

Then followed the smaller dishes :

Tiny cakes as white and delicate as ladies' fingers ;

Birds' nests made of spun sugar (and in the nests were eggs of marsh-mallow, and in each egg was a tiny chicken made of caramel !) ;

Figs and dates from the desert ;

Other fruits, in and out of season ;

Syrups and preserves fetched from the four corners of the world ;

Wines cooled in snow from the distant mountains.

One might fill pages merely by setting down the names of all the delicacies.

Each dish was brought in by the servants in a kind of procession, headed by the Master-Cook, looking as grand and solemn as an archbishop, for he was a grave and dignified person, and of course he had a great responsibility. The guests were served by little page-boys of noble birth,

dressed in the liveries of their masters, and these pages handed the dishes and the wines most politely on their bended knees as they had been taught to do.

So the guests enjoyed themselves, and the fiddlers played, and the King laughed at everything everybody said, because he was in a mighty good humour, and the bright afternoon sun, shining through the western windows, lighted up the rich hangings on the walls, and flashed upon the jewels on fair ladies' fingers, and fell upon the marble pavement in a pool of gold.

And then, you know, when the merriment was at its height, something happened! There was a sudden cry, and a harsh voice, like the croaking of a raven, sounded through the room.

"Be merry, my lords and ladies," cried the voice. "Laugh while you may, but remember that tears may follow laughter."

A hush fell upon all the brilliant assembly. The Queen turned pale and shuddered. The King rose hurriedly from his place, and he and all the guests turned to look at the strange figure that had suddenly appeared in the doorway.

They saw an old woman bent almost double with age, her grey head with matted hair sunk deep between her shoulders. Her face was white and twisted with anger, and her green eyes flashed spitefully.

Slowly she advanced towards the dais, and stretching out her arm, pointed her finger at the gold plates and the gold caskets set before the fairy godmothers. "There's one," said she, with a harsh laugh, "there's two, there's twelve! Did you not know, O King, that there were thirteen wise women in your kingdom, and the thirteenth the wisest and most powerful of all ? Where, then, is the plate and the casket set for me ? "

The King began to make excuses, imploring the angry old fairy to forgive him for his neglect, and begging her to sit down and join them in their festivities. " For," said he, " I am sure you are very welcome."

" Is it so, indeed ? " said the thirteenth fairy. " I am not too late, then, though the feast is all but done. I shall eat off silver while my sisters eat off gold, and there is no curiously-shaped casket for me. No matter, I am content, because I am in time, and I shall dower the Princess with the gift which I have brought for her ! " And here the spiteful creature uttered another of her sneering laughs, which made the blood of all the guests run cold.

By dint of much coaxing the King at last managed to persuade her to sit down, and the feast proceeded. But a chill had been cast over the assembly, and nothing was quite the same as it had been before. The old crone muttered and mouthed over her food, now and again smiling to herself as though she were cherishing some secret and evil triumph. The other fairies cast anxious glances at her, for they feared her malice, and the youngest fairy of all, who happened to be seated at the end of the table, presently rose up quietly from her place and, stealing away, hid herself behind the arras. And nobody saw her go, nor did a single person remark upon her absence.

CHAPTER IV

AND now came the time for the most important part of the ceremony, when the fairy godmothers should declare their gifts to the royal child. All this time the little Princess Briar-Rose had been quietly sleeping in her cradle in the nursery, watched over by an old servant who had tended her mother as a child. Now the King gave orders for the baby to be brought into the banqueting hall. The guests ceased their laughter and talk, and the musicians laid by their instruments.

So the sleeping child was brought and placed in her mother's arms. How tenderly she clasped the baby to her breast, bending over it as though to shield it from all harm. So sweet a sight should have touched the hardest heart, and indeed there was only one person in the room who remained unmoved, and that was the spiteful and jealous fairy, who looked up and bared her yellow teeth in a sneering grin.

"Queen," said she, "your face is pale and your lips tremble. What is it that you fear on this day of the giving of gifts?"

But the Queen shuddered and was silent.

Then a fairy rose in her place and said—

"I will begin. My gift to the Princess Briar-Rose is the gift of Beauty. She shall have eyes like stars, and hair as bright as the sunshine of the spring day on which she was born, and cheeks as fresh and fair as the petals of the flower from which she takes her name. None shall surpass her in loveliness."

Then the second fairy rose in her turn and said: "After Beauty, Wit. The Princess shall be cleverer than any ordinary mortal could ever hope to be."

"I give her Virtue," said the third. And the Queen nodded her head and smiled, for though she esteemed beauty and cleverness, she knew that neither was of any worth without goodness of heart.

So all the fairies in turn named the gift which they had brought for Briar-Rose. The fourth said that whatever the Princess put her hand to, she should do with the most exquisite grace; the fifth, that she should sing like a nightingale; the sixth that she should dance as lightly as a

fairy, and so on until she had nearly all the virtues and accomplishments which even a King might desire for his daughter. But as yet, the spiteful old fairy had not said a word.

At last she rose and cast an evil glance round.

"Have you all finished?" said she. "Hear, then, my wish. On the day when she reaches her fifteenth birthday, the Princess shall prick her finger with the spindle of a spinning-wheel, and shall immediately die!"

This terrible prophecy made the whole company shudder. The Queen gave a cry and hugged the sleeping baby still closer to her breast.

"No, no! Have pity!" she cried. "Call down your dreadful fate on my head if you will, but do not harm this innocent child."

At this mournful appeal there was hardly one of the guests who could keep from tears, but the old crone only mumbled to herself as though she were uttering a spell. Then the King leapt to his feet, his hand at the jewelled hilt of the dagger that hung at his girdle. In another moment he might have stretched the wicked creature lifeless at his feet, but before he could draw the weapon from its sheath, another voice arrested him.

"Stay your hand, O King, lest even worse befall. No mortal may strike at a fairy and go unpunished. And, for the rest, take comfort, for your daughter shall not die!"

Then the twelfth fairy stepped out from behind the arras where she had been hidden. "My gift is still to come," she continued. "As far as I can, I will undo the mischief which my sister has done. It is true that I have not the power to prevent altogether what she has decreed. The Princess shall, indeed, prick her finger with the spindle of the spinning-wheel on the day when she attains her fifteenth year ; but instead of dying she shall fall into a deep sleep ; and this sleep shall last for a hundred years, and when that time is past, a King's son shall come to waken her."

CHAPTER V

SO the worst was averted, but the fate of the poor little Princess was still terrible enough, and it was only to be expected that the King should do his best to prevent the prophecy from coming to fulfilment.

The first thing he did was to summon all the magicians of his own and neighbouring countries, promising a rich reward to the one who could show him a way to defeat the old fairy's malice. The magicians came in scores, some with long beards reaching to their feet, some without any beards at all, some with bald heads, and some with matted hair that looked as though it had not been combed for centuries. For days there were so many magicians about the palace that they were commoner than cats, and it was impossible to enter any room without surprising one or the other of them, sitting in deep reflection and looking as wise as only a magician can look. But nothing came of their thinking, and one after the other they gave up the task and departed, having first asked for their travelling expenses.

At last there came a wizard who was wiser and more venerable than all the rest, and when he heard what was required of him he said he would go home and consult his secret books which contained the magic lore of all the ages, and which had been written by the greatest of all the magicians, Merlin himself.

Home, then, he went, to his cell, which was in a rocky cliff on the side of a mountain, and having uttered the word of power which unlocked the massive door, he entered and prepared to begin his researches.

Now the books of magic lore which Merlin had written were in many volumes, and everything in them was set down in alphabetical order, so that it could be found easily. The old wizard, therefore, turned first of all to the word *Princess*. Five hundred pages were devoted to this subject,

and, truly, there was a great deal of very interesting information.   As thus :—

PRINCESS : How to transform Goosegirl into.

Spell for causing Princess to be surrounded with high walls of bronze, which may by no means be broken down except by the notes of a certain trumpet (*q.v.*).

(Now *q.v.* are the first letters of two magic words which are to be found in all dictionaries and encyclopædias to this day).

PRINCESS : Enchanted ring for.

A new and improved method by which she may be changed into a fawn together with any members of her family according to desire, and all of them transformed back again into their proper shape.

PRINCESS : An excellent device for causing a Princess to grow tall or short by eating of a mushroom, with directions how to find the place where the mushroom grows, and precautions to be taken lest by over-much nibbling she disappear altogether.

And so on.   But there was never a word about how to prevent a Princess from falling into a charmed sleep through pricking her finger with the spindle of a spinning-wheel.

So when he had read all through the five hundred pages, the venerable wizard turned to the word *Sleep*, in the hope that he would meet with better fortune.

And there was much reliable information under this heading also.   There were recipes for potent drugs which would cause sleep, and for still more potent drugs which would prevent people from going to sleep, and when the wizard came to this last he cried out eagerly, for he thought that he had succeeded in his quest, until he read on and discovered that the spell described was only for use on wicked Queens who had shamefully ill-used their step-children. It is very easy to make a mistake in magic, for it is a most complicated science.

By the time he had read through the two hundred pages devoted to the word *Sleep*, the venerable wizard was very uneasy, but he was a persevering person and he did not abandon his endeavours. Merlin's wise books having failed him, he cast about for other means to learn what he desired, and consulted his oracle.

Now his oracle was a stuffed crocodile hanging from the ceiling, and a voice came from it which told him to repeat the magic formula.

The magic formula is a sentence made up of all the sounds that are left out of ordinary speech, and it is a fearsome thing to listen to. It is also very exhausting to say, and after the venerable wizard had repeated it, he was obliged to rest for several hours. Then he rose again and drew pentagons on the rocky floor of his cave, and crossed triangles and circles bordered with all the signs of the Zodiac. And he stood in the middle of the pentagons and the crossed triangles and the circles and went through all sorts of strange and secret rites, but all to no purpose.

But still he would not give up trying ; and he went to mysterious places in the woods and gathered strange herbs in the dark of the moon. And, returning home, he cast the herbs into a brazier and they burnt with flames of many colours, giving out clouds of dense smoke and a most horrible smell. Then, as these exercises did not bring

him the result he desired, he gazed into crystals and poured ink into the palm of his hand, and did all the other things that he had learnt to do in all the years since he was apprenticed to magic as a very small boy.

And just as he was going to give up the quest in despair, a thought came into his head, and he cried aloud for joy, for he knew he had discovered what he sought. This shows how even the most difficult things may be attained by perseverance and patience.

At the top of his speed he hastened back to the palace and asked an audience of the King. This was immediately granted, for, to tell the truth, the King was awaiting his return with considerable anxiety.

"Well," said he, "have you succeeded in finding a way?"

"I have," answered the venerable wizard. "My arts have not failed me!" And he handed the King a piece of parchment on which were written the following words. They were written in Latin to make them look more important, but very likely it was not good Latin, for the venerable wizard had been apprenticed to his trade at an early age, and in consequence his classical education had been somewhat neglected. But this was the meaning of them:

> Shall spindle prick ?—then spindle burn,
> No thread weave and no wheel turn ;
> If there's no spindle and there's no wheel,
> Then no finger the spindle can feel.

The King slapped his thigh for joy. " Why, of course ! "
said he. " How is it that I did not myself think of such
a simple solution ? It seems to me, Wizard, that you have
easily earned your thousand crowns ! "

" Ah, Majesty," the wizard made answer, " all things
are simple when once you know them."

And in this he was quite right.

CHAPTER VI

THE King lost no time in putting the wizard's counsel into effect. The very next day he caused a proclamation to be written, and ordered copies of it to be fixed on all the church doors, and in all the public places of every town in his kingdom. This is the way the proclamation read :

WHEREAS a certain malicious fairy, forgetful of the duties she owes to the most high and puissant King and Queen, rightful sovereigns of these realms, and to the Princess Briar-Rose, their dearly loved daughter, has, of malice aforethought, and with intent to work grievous bodily harm to the person of the said Princess, in the presence of the said most puissant Sovereigns and of divers of their loyal subjects made and uttered a prophecy, to wit : that the said Princess shall in her fifteenth year prick her finger with the spindle of a spinning-wheel, and that a certain dire misfortune shall fall upon her because of that injury, to the sorrow of her loving parents : NOW BE IT DECREED That all spinning-wheels or instruments of spinning whatsoever, in the possession of any subjects of the King's most excellent Majesty, whether they be worked by hand or by treadle or by any other device, together with all spindles, shuttles, bobbins, and all other accessories or appurtenances thereunto belonging, shall forthwith be rendered up to the officers of the King's most excellent Majesty appointed to receive them. AND BE IT FURTHER DECREED That if any person or persons fail to observe or obey this edict or ordinance by unlawfully retaining any instrument of spinning or accessory thereunto, such persons shall be dealt with according to the full rigour of the law, and shall suffer the penalty of death.

Given under our royal hand and seal.

The issue of this proclamation caused a great deal of interest and excitement throughout the kingdom. All the people came out of their houses to gaze at it, for they had never seen its like before, and though very few of them knew how to read they realised that it must mean something very important. So they sent for clerks and scholars to read it to them, paying a penny apiece for the service, which pennies, the clerks and scholars, being usually extraordinarily needy persons, were very glad to earn. It usually took about three hours to read the proclamation and to explain it ; and one must admit that it might have been expressed in fewer words. To do so, however, would not have been dignified, for this proclamation was what is called a legal instrument.

The very next day into each town and village of the kingdom the King's officers came riding. Before them went a trumpeter who stopped at the head of each street and blew a loud call. Having thus commanded attention he marched past the houses calling in a loud voice :

"Bring out your spinning-wheels. Bring out your spinning-wheels ! "

So the people brought them out, not without grumbling, for a spinning-wheel is a very useful thing to have in a house, and in those days people spun and wove their own cloth to make their clothes. But they were afraid to disobey the King's order.

And the spinning-wheels were of all shapes and sizes, some of them new and some of them hundreds of years old, and there was hardly a house that did not possess one of some kind or another. They were all collected together and loaded into waggons and taken to the capital, where

they were piled up into an immense heap in the public   49
square.

Then the King and Queen and all the court came out
and watched while the big heap was set on fire.   The
people came out to watch too in their thousands, and a
very fine sight it was to see the enormous flames shooting
up into the air and to hear the crackle and hiss of the
burning wood that sounded like the discharge of a hundred
muskets.

The King laughed aloud in his relief, and even the
Queen smiled, while the little Princess Briar-Rose, who was
held up to a window of the palace to see the bonfire,
stretched out her arms to the pretty flames and crowed.
But the people were not very much amused by the sight
because they were their spinning-wheels which were being
burnt.

50   "I've had my wheel for twenty years," said one woman, "and now I've none at all, and how on earth I can

to find breeches for!"

"Five silver crowns my wheel cost my good man last Candlemass," said another, "and there it goes up in flames and smoke."

"What is a wheel if the burning of it saves our little Princess?" quoth a third. "Come, cheer up, Mother, the King has reason for what he does and he will not see us want."

And this man was right. The King had no wish to oppress his subjects, for no sooner was the pile reduced to ashes than he caused another proclamation to be issued, saying that the owner of every spinning-wheel should be paid for its loss. And not only so, but the King told his merchants to buy spun yarn from neighbouring countries so that the people might be able to weave, even though they could not spin.

CHAPTER VII

THE little Princess Briar-Rose, of course, knew nothing of the strange events that had happened at the feast of her christening, and the King gave orders that nobody should even mention the subject to her. It is not a pleasant thing to know that the fairies have decreed that one shall fall asleep for a hundred years on one's fifteenth birthday, even though one is to be awakened by a handsome Prince at the end of that time. So all the lords-in-waiting and the ladies-in-waiting had to be very careful and discreet. If they told the Princess a story, they had to keep the word "spinning" out of it; and if they showed her a book they had to take pains to see it did not contain a picture of a spinning-wheel, or any reference to a distaff or spindle, lest she should ask what they were. The King's Customs officers, on the boundaries of the kingdom, had to examine every waggon-load of merchandise that came into the country for fear it should contain a spinning-wheel; and if anybody was found trying to smuggle one in he was brought before the judges and punished.

By these devices the King felt certain that he had averted the fate laid upon his daughter.

But the promises of the other wise women were fulfilled to the letter, for the young Princess grew up to be the most beautiful, gifted and gracious maiden in all the world. That, at any rate, was what everybody in the palace said,

from the lords and ladies down to the scullions in the
kitchen, and although people are inclined sometimes to
flatter Royalty, in this case there was reason for their
admiration.

To begin with, the Princess was as lovely as a spring
morning, with eyes of the purest, softest blue, and hair in
which the rays of the sun seemed to be entangled. When
she came into a room people stopped whatever they were
doing to look at her, and everyone felt happier because she
was there.

And her cleverness! She never had any trouble with her letters or her multiplication table. She could cipher as easily as she could spell; she knew the history of her own country and of every country round it; and nobody could puzzle her with the hardest question in geography. She could sew and embroider, and knit and paint and draw;

she studied mathematics and botany and astronomy and even law. In short, there was no end to her knowledge, and all because she had those fairies for her godmothers.

Besides this, there were all her other accomplishments; she could play on all sorts of musical instruments, as, for instance, fiddle and zither, large harp and jew's-harp, church organ and mouth organ, flute and penny-whistle, and even on the nursery comb ; she could sing like a nightingale and dance

And yet she was never conceited or puffed-up, as some good-looking and accomplished people are apt to be. On the contrary, she was always sweet-tempered and modest, and for this reason she was loved. People may admire

good looks and a graceful deportment, and they may
respect ability, but it is only sweetness of nature and
goodness of heart that can win love. And these things
were the gift of the third fairy.

So the years passed, and at last came the day when the Princess Briar-Rose was fifteen years of age.

What a day that was! Everybody came to wish her many happy returns, and she had so many presents that at least a dozen servants were kept busy unwrapping the parcels. The King gave her a white pony with a saddle of red velvet, and bridle and stirrups of gold, while the Queen's present was a beautiful and costly necklace of pearls. Even the boy who turned the spit in the kitchen brought her something, and though it was only a little wooden shoe which he had carved with his own hands, the

Princess prized it just as much as though it had been made
of gold.

The only person who was not happy on the Princess's birthday was the Queen, and she went about with a pale face and a look of great anxiety.

"Come, come, my love," said the King, "what is the matter with you? Surely you are not thinking of that foolish old prophecy!"

"How can I help thinking about it?" the Queen answered. "I have not been able to get it out of my mind for fifteen years, and now that the day has come I am afraid."

"Make your mind easy," said the King. "Nothing is going to happen. Why, there's not a spinning-wheel within a hundred miles. I have taken good care of that!" And he went away chuckling, to attend a meeting of his Cabinet. But the Queen shook her head.

Now while the King and Queen were talking, the Princess Briar-Rose was wandering about in the castle, visiting room after room, as she had done many times before. The castle was so big that a stranger might easily have been lost in its maze of stairways and corridors, but Briar-Rose knew every part of it quite well, from the great kitchens below ground, where on feast days a score of cooks prepared the dinner for hundreds of guests, to the topmost turret above the battlements, where the sentries kept watch with their pikes on their shoulders. There was only one part of the castle which Briar-Rose had never explored, and that was an ancient tower which rose from the eastern end. The door of that tower was always locked, and

although the Princess had often tried to find the key she had never succeeded. The servants told her that the tower had not been inhabited for nearly a hundred years, and it had never been entered within the memory of anybody in the castle.

To-day Briar-Rose flitted restlessly from place to place. She peeped into the kitchen and saw the kitchen boys turning the spits on which whole oxen were being roasted. Then she went into the empty throne room and saw the golden thrones side by side upon the dais, and the rich tapestry, glowing with all the colours of the rainbow, on the walls. After that she mounted to the battlements from which she could see over miles and miles of her father's kingdom, and not content with that, she ran up the

staircases into the turrets and looked through their narrow
slits of windows upon the courtyard below, so far down
that the people walking therein seemed no bigger than
mice. And then she came down again and continued her
wanderings, searching in all sorts of out-of-the-way corners,
until at last she found herself before the door of the
ancient tower into which she had never been. And as she
looked at the door, she gave a start of surprise and then
a cry of joy.

There was a key in the lock.

CHAPTER VIII

IT was a rusty key, and Briar-Rose was afraid that she might not be able to turn it, but to her surprise it turned quite easily. The heavy door swung inward on its ancient hinges with many a creak and groan, and she found herself in a little dark room thickly carpeted with the dust of years. From this room a winding staircase led upward, and Briar-Rose was just about to climb the stair when a sudden noise made her start back in alarm.

Whirr ! There was a beating of wings, a flurry and a scuffle, and past her face flew a dark shape, with gleaming, yellow eyes. It was only an owl who was hiding in the

tower out of the sunlight, but he gave poor Briar-Rose a great fright, and she was in two minds whether to turn back or not, but the winding staircase looked very inviting and she wanted to see whither it led, so gathering up her skirts to avoid any creepy things that might be crawling about, she ran up the stairway as fast as she could, round and round until she reached the top. There she came upon another door.

In this door also was a rusty key, and Briar-Rose turned it as easily as she had turned the first. Then she pushed open the door and entered.

She found herself in a small room lighted by narrow windows. Beneath one of these windows was a couch, and in front of it sat an old woman with a spinning-wheel.

"Good-morrow, Motherkin," said the Princess. "What are you doing?"

"I am spinning, my pretty child," answered the old woman without ceasing her work.

"Spinning?" asked the Princess. "Oh, do let me see! What is that thing which goes round so merrily?"

"That is the spinning-wheel," said the old woman. "Why, child, you speak as though you had never seen such a thing before."

"Indeed, I have not," said the Princess. "How interesting it is! I wonder whether I could do it as well as you. Will you let me try?"

"Why, of course," said the old woman, "every young girl should know how to spin. Here you are, my dear," and she gave Briar-Rose the spindle.

Now whether the Princess in her eagerness to seize the

spindle grasped it too roughly, or whether it was just because
the fairy had ordained that it should be so, I do not know,
but anyhow the sharp iron point pricked her hand, and
immediately she fell backward on to the couch in a deep
sleep.

And in that very moment sleep fell upon every man,
woman and child in the castle, and upon every living thing
within its gates. The King, who was sitting at the
Council-board with his ministers, stopped speaking in the
middle of a sentence, and remained with his mouth open,
in the act of uttering a word, and nobody remarked the
strangeness of his conduct, for all his ministers were asleep
too, just as they sat. Outside the door the sentry leaned
upon his pike. In the Queen's chamber the ladies-in-
waiting fell into a profound slumber in the very midst
of what they were doing—one as she was hemming a
handkerchief, another over her embroidery, still another
while she was talking to her parrot. The Queen slept in
her chair, and a little page-boy who was singing fell asleep
in the middle of a note.

All through the castle the charmed slumber spread.
Courtiers, officers, stewards, cooks, errand-boys, soldiers,
beadles, nay the very horses in the stables and the dogs in
their kennels were stricken motionless as though they were
dead. The flies ceased to buzz at the windows and the
pigeons to coo upon the roof. In the great kitchen the
scullions fell asleep as they were washing up the dishes,
and a cook in the very act of boxing the ears of a
kitchen-knave.

But not for a hundred years would he feel that blow,
or be able to utter the cry that was on the tip of his

tongue.   The dog fell asleep under the table as he was gnawing a bone; the cat in front of a mouse-hole, the

mouse itself on the other side of the skirting-board, with
its little sharp nose outstretched to sniff the air suspiciously.

Even the spits which were turning at the fire, laden with partridges and pheasants cooking for the Princess's birthday feast—even they ceased to turn, and the very fire stopped flickering and the flames sank down.

A deep silence fell over the castle. In the fields the lambs ceased to bleat, the horses to neigh and the cows to low. The birds in the trees were silent. One moment the air was full of the music of their twittering ; the next, all was as still as in a desert. The very wind dropped to sleep in the woods ; not a leaf stirred, and the white clouds were motionless in the sky.

*　　*　　*　　*　　*　　*

So sleep fell upon the enchanted castle and upon all within it, because of the Princess Briar-Rose, who lay there on her couch in the ancient tower waiting till the hundred years should be past and the Prince should come to waken her.

And all round the castle there grew up a hedge of thorn, tangled with ivy, woodbine and creeping plants, so dense that from a distance it seemed like a little wood. Higher and higher it grew, closing round the castle like a wall until all that could be seen was the top of the highest tower, and the flagstaff from which the royal standard hung limp and motionless.

And the years went by, each with its changing seasons. Spring came and brought to the fields and woods outside the new life of leaf and flower. The trees awoke from their winter sleep and clothed themselves gloriously in

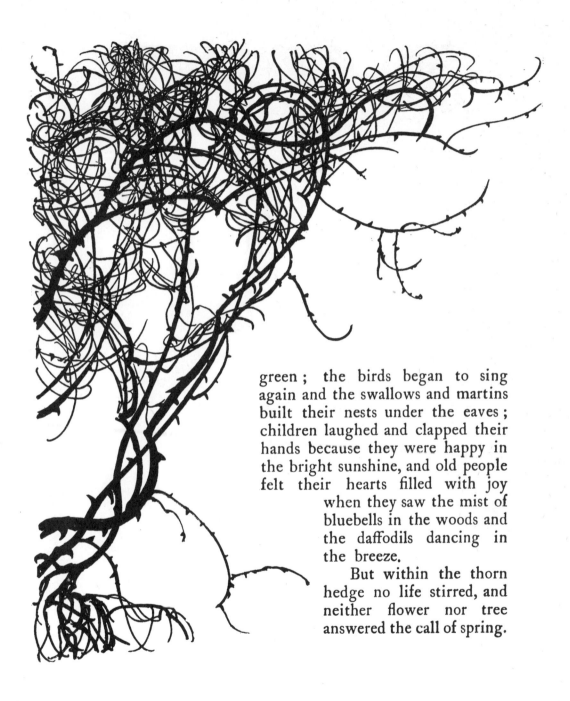

green ; the birds began to sing again and the swallows and martins built their nests under the eaves ; children laughed and clapped their hands because they were happy in the bright sunshine, and old people felt their hearts filled with joy when they saw the mist of bluebells in the woods and the daffodils dancing in the breeze.

But within the thorn hedge no life stirred, and neither flower nor tree answered the call of spring.

As time went on, the people who were young when
the palace was enchanted grew old and died, but they
never forgot the prophecy that one of these days the
sleeping Princess should awaken ; and they told the story
to their children, who told it in their turn, changing it a
little because it was only a tale to them.   And so, after
many years, the legend spread abroad to neighbouring
countries, and many a young prince dreamed that it was he
who was destined to break the spell and waken the sleeping
Princess.

Now and again one would take the quest upon him
and try to force his way through the thick hedge.   But no
one succeeded.   The sharp thorns gripped the unhappy
young men like clutching hands, and held them fast, so that
they could neither go forward nor back, and they perished
miserably.   Their bones, whitened by the sun and wind,
remained there as a warning for all to see, and the
creeping plants grew over them.

CHAPTER IX

A HUNDRED years passed away. At the end of that time it happened one day that a young Prince who was hunting in the neighbourhood caught sight of the towers of the enchanted castle rising above the dense forest. He had never been in that part of the country before, and had heard nothing of the story of the Sleeping Princess, so he asked the first people he met what those towers were, and to whom the castle belonged.

Everybody told him a different tale. One said that it was an old castle haunted by spirits; another, that it was a meeting-place for all the witches and sorcerers in the land, who gathered there to practise their secret rites.

"No, no," said a third. "That castle is the home of a giant, and all the people in these parts are very much afraid of him, so I have been told, because he steals their cattle and their crops, and even carries off their children to be his servants. And they cannot go to the rescue of those he has imprisoned in this way, because of the forest all round the castle, which is so dense that nobody can force his way through.

And so they went on, one saying one thing, and one another, for each repeated what he had heard. At last an old peasant stepped forward.

"Fifty years ago, my Prince," said he, "my father told me the story of that castle, and since he was born in these parts, I think it was the true story, and I will tell it you if you would like to hear it."

The Prince nodded eagerly, and the old man went on :

"My father said that years before he himself was born a King and Queen lived in the castle with their daughter, the most beautiful Princess that ever was seen. In some way or other they angered the fairies, who put a spell upon the place and upon every one within it, so that they fell into a deep sleep. My father said that this sleep would last a hundred years, but at the end of that time a King's son should come and waken the beautiful Princess and make her his bride."

When the young Prince heard these words he felt his heart beat quickly. Something seemed to tell him that he and no other was the King's son who was destined to remove the spell, and he cried : " Show me the way to the castle, for I will take this adventure upon me."

But the old man shook his head. " I have not yet told you all, my Prince. Many are the young men who have tried to force their way through the thick wood that guards the enchanted castle. Each of them thought that he, and he alone, was destined to awaken the Sleeping Beauty, and each of them set out with high hopes ; but none of them all came back, and their bones, whitened by the wind and rain, lie among the thorns of the thick

hedge, a fearful warning to the venturesome. I pray you, therefore, my Prince, do nothing rash, but think well before you take upon yourself this perilous quest."

"What," cried the Prince with flashing eyes, "shall I hold back when others have dared? This very hour I will attempt to enter the castle, and if I do not return, carry home the news of how I have died."

Then without paying any heed to the words of those who would prevent him from rushing into such danger, the eager young man set out, his heart on fire with thoughts of love and glory. Nobody showed him the way, but he could see the towers of the castle rising above the distant wood, and when he entered the wood itself, and the towers were hidden, each path he took led him nearer to the place where he would be.

At last he came to an open glade, and there before him was a tangled hedge of thorn, stretching in either direction as far as the eye could see.

CHAPTER X

AND now, as the Prince drew nearer, he could see that the story he had heard about that terrible place was true, for held in the tangle of briar were the bones of many unhappy young men who had tried to force their way through to the castle. Rags and tatters of their finery hung upon the great thorns that pointed menacingly like sharp claws. Here and there upon the ground beneath lay pieces of rusty armour, a helmet surrounded by a coronet of gold that once had belonged to a King's son, a shield with a Prince's device, a sword with jewel-encrusted hilt worth a King's ransom. There they lay, all disregarded among the blanched bones upon the grass, and the ground-ivy spread out its leaves to cover them.

Not a sound broke the deep and awful silence. No bird sang, no insect droned ; there was no scurry of woodland creatures among the leaves, no sigh of wind in the trees. In all that place only the thorn hedge seemed threateningly alive, waiting to destroy the intruder who should attempt to force the secret it guarded.

Who would blame the Prince if for a moment his heart had almost failed him ? There was no gap in that hedge, and the great thorns were sharp as dagger blades to stab his flesh. But if the Prince hesitated it was not for long.

"Have I come so far to turn back now?" he thought. "These others who have died were brave men, and though they failed, with a courage as great as theirs I may succeed." And without wasting another moment the Prince began to force his way through the hedge.

And now he noticed with surprise that those thorns which looked so sharp and cruel became soft as thistle-down as soon as he touched them, and the trailing bramble branches did not entangle him but bent aside at his touch as though they had been stems of grass. The hedge opened before him, and as he went through it pink blossoms of wild roses bloomed on the branches, until the tangled wall became a mass of flowers.

At last the Prince found himself on the other side of the hedge in the gardens of the castle. Before him he could see the high towers and turrets bathed in the fresh light of the morning sun, and as he hastened towards them he noticed that the gardens were as trim and tidy as though they had just been tended by the gardeners. There was no moss or weed upon the smooth paths, the turf on the lawns was as short and firm as though it had just been mown, and in the flower-beds everything was in the most careful order. Spring flowers were blooming there, but they bowed their heads upon their stalks, and even the trees seemed to hang their arms as though asleep.

Everywhere there was the same deep silence. The air, which should have been full of the twittering of birds, was heavy and languorous. There was no flutter of butter-fly-wings or darting of flies; the fountains on the lawns were not playing, and as the Prince glanced over the edge

of the marble basin of one of them he could see the goldfish beneath the water-lily leaves lying still, with never a wave of the tail or flicker of fin.

So he went on over the lawns and terraces and never a waking thing did he see, but when he came to the court-yard he saw a soldier standing there, leaning on his pike with his head bent upon his chest. At first the Prince

thought that he was dead, but his cheek was fresh and
ruddy and it was quite plain to see that he was merely
asleep. In the courtyard itself were other human forms,
all still and silent. A row of pikemen leaned against the
wall and in front of them, stretched out upon the ground,
snored the sergeant who had been drilling them when the
spell came upon the castle. A young squire, with a sleeping

hawk upon his wrist, slept leaning against a sleeping horse which he had been about to mount. Near by lay a page with a hound in leash, both sleeping as soundly as though they never would awake, and through a window in the stables the Prince saw a groom lying with a straw in his mouth.

In the stables themselves a like condition of things prevailed. The horses slept at their stalls with their noses to the mangers, standing on their four legs just as they were when they were enchanted a hundred years before, and on the back of one of them sat the stable-cat. Here and there upon the ground lay grooms and ostlers, fast asleep among the straw.

From the stables the Prince made his way to the great kitchen where he saw equally strange sights, and he could not help smiling when he came upon the cook with her hand still outstretched to clout the head of the unhappy scullion whom she had by the ear. Before the fires hung the spitted partridges and fowls that were cooking for the Princess's birthday feast, and at the table a maid had fallen asleep with her hands in a large trough full of dough. She had been making the pastry for a pie when the sleep fell upon her, and by her side was another maid who had been plucking a black hen. At the sink a kitchen-knave was leaning over the pot he had been scouring.

Then the Prince went out into the great hall and saw the courtiers asleep in the window alcoves, or stretched out upon the polished floor. Everywhere was a silence so profound that the Prince was almost alarmed to hear his own breathing, and the beating of his heart sounded like a muffled drum. On and on he went, through rooms and corridors, up staircases and down staircases, into the Queen's chamber where he saw the Queen and her ladies as still and silent as the rest ; one of those ladies had been reading to the Queen at the moment when the charmed sleep fell upon the castle, and the book, a History of Troy, still lay open on her lap. Then the Prince went into the King's room where his Majesty sat with his ministers of state round the Council board. He almost lingered there, for it was very curious to see those nobles as quiet and motionless as though they had been waxworks in a show. Some of them were frowning as though in deep thought, and some smiling as though they had suddenly remembered something clever to say. The King himself, at the head of the Council table, had evidently fallen asleep in the very midst of a speech, for his arm lay outstretched on the table with pointing finger, and, by his side, his secretary's fingers still held the pen with which he was inscribing on a roll of parchment the royal words.

So the Prince hurried through the castle from top to bottom until he had glanced into every room and opened every door. And still he knew that there was something more to see, for nowhere had he come across the sleeping Princess. Many maidens he had seen of surpassing beauty, but his heart told him that none of them all was the maiden whom he had come to awaken.

Down he went into the courtyard again and found another stairway which led to the battlements. There stood the watchmen whose duty it was to look out over the country and report the arrival of travellers, but they, too, were all asleep, though one of them had his horn in his hand as though he had been about to blow it when he was suddenly overcome by the charmed slumber.

From the battlements the Prince climbed, in turn, into each of the turrets, but there was nobody in them at all, and no living thing except the owls asleep in the crevices of the walls, and the bats that hung head downward from the rafters. Now only one small turret remained to be explored. It was the oldest of the turrets, almost a ruin, and plainly long unused, for the iron door was rusty and the ivy trailed about the walls.

The Prince approached it with a beating heart, for there he knew he should find what he sought. He threw open the creaking door; with impatient feet he mounted the crazy, winding stair, opened the door at the top and entered a little dark room.

And then—and then he started forward with a cry of joy and wonder, for lying on the couch below the narrow window he saw the Princess.

She was lying upon a couch with her lovely hair spread out like a stream of gold; and, oh! no words can tell how beautiful she was. Softly the Prince came near and bent over her. He touched her hand; it was warm as in life, but she did not stir. No sound of breathing came from her parted lips, fresh and sweet as the petals of a rose; her eyes were closed.

For a long time the Prince stood and gazed upon her, for never in all his life had he seen a maiden so lovely. Then suddenly he bent down and kissed her lips.

That was the end of the enchantment. The Princess's

eyelids quivered; languidly she moved her head and stretched out her arms. Her eyes opened and she smiled.

"Is it you, my Prince?" she said. "How long you have kept me waiting!"

CHAPTER XI

IN that very moment the charm was broken and the castle awoke.

Instead of the profound silence there came a hustle and confusion of noise. Clocks began to strike, doors began to slam, dogs began to bark, cocks began to crow and hens to cluck ; a breeze sprang up outside and set the branches of the trees swaying and creaking ; the doves began to coo upon the roofs, the swallows to twitter under the eaves, flies came out and buzzed about the window, mice squeaked in the wainscot and ran scampering along the rafters. The fountain in the garden leapt up sixty feet into the air, and the goldfish swam among the water-lily leaves ; ants left their nests and foraged about the paths, the butterflies danced and fluttered over the flowers, which lifted their heads as though to drink in the rays of the sun. In every tree in the garden a thrush woke up and began to sing ; sparrows chirped, jays screamed, blue-tits chattered, and the chiff-chaff uttered his strange note. In the woods a cuckoo called and blackbird fluted to blackbird in the hedge. In the stables the horses awoke and champed at their stalls ; the cat jumped down and ran after a mouse which crept out from under the straw. The sentry at the courtyard gate woke up and rubbed his eyes and came smartly to attention, looking round uneasily, for he thought he had only been asleep for a few minutes and was afraid that somebody

might have seen him who would report him to the sergeant.
The pikemen also woke with a start, and the sergeant woke
too, and bellowed an order in a loud and angry voice, for he
was ashamed of himself for sleeping in front of his men.

The young squire who was going hawking fitted his falcon's hood and mounted his steed; the page-boy with the hound went off to his master. On the topmost tower of the castle the royal standard, which had been drooping against the flagstaff, filled out and waved freely in the breeze.

The hedge which had grown up to surround the enchanted castle broke in and disappeared; peacocks squalled and strutted on the lawns, martins flitted to and from their nests under the eaves, pigs began to grunt, oxen to low, sheep to bleat, rooks to caw and children to laugh and sing. In short, all the sounds which we hear every day and all the time and never notice, began again and seemed so loud in contrast to the deadly silence that they almost cracked the ears.

And in every room in the castle the people who had been lying asleep for a hundred years woke up and went on with what they had been doing just as though nothing had happened. In the kitchen the flames of the fire leapt up with a hiss and a roar. The kettle began to boil, the stew-pot to bubble, and the meat before the fire to steam and hiss as the little boy turned the spit.

"Take that," cried the cook, giving the scullion the clout she had promised a hundred years before. "Take that for a lazy knave."

"Goodness," yawned the maid who had been plucking the black hen; "I wonder what made me drop off to sleep like that? Well, well, it's to be hoped the cook didn't see me!" And my word, how she made the feathers fly!

Miaou! cried the cat in disgust as he made a pounce at the mouse-hole he had been watching, for the little mouse

who had poked his nose out a hundred years before drew it
back like a flash and scampered away.

"Dear me!" said the servant who was washing the dishes; "I do believe I have been to sleep with this crock in my hand. It's a mercy I didn't let it fall!" And he went on with his scouring. It was the same thing in the dairy where the maids had fallen asleep while they were skimming the cream and churning the butter. And the cream was not sour for all that a hundred years had passed,

nor was the butter rank.   But a fly which had been sleeping on the edge of one of the milk-pans woke up and flew down to taste the milk, and fell in and was drowned, so he was

none the better because the spell had been taken off the castle.

In the Queen's ante-chamber the maids-of-honour and the ladies-in-waiting sat up and yawned and stretched themselves. Each one of them thought that she was the only one who had fallen asleep, and they all began to explain at the same time that they had only closed their eyes for forty seconds. "It was the heat," they all said to each other. "The sun is very hot for this time of year."

In the King's council chamber the King and all his ministers woke up with a start. The ministers rubbed their eyes and looked very sheepish, for each of them thought that he was alone in being caught napping.

"Your Majesty was saying . . . ?" said the Prime Minister respectfully, leaning forward.

"I was saying . . ." said the King. "What was I saying ?" And he stretched out his arms and yawned. "I crave your pardon, my lords. I do believe I've been asleep. Heigho ! but my joints are stiff."

"It was but an after-dinner nap," said the Prime Minister. "Your Majesty is overspent with the hard hunting yesterday. Is it your Majesty's will that we should proceed with our business, or shall the Council rise until to-morrow ? "

"Go on, my lords, go on," cried the King heartily. "My little nap has wonderfully refreshed me. What say you, shall we pass that bill we were discussing a few minutes ago ? "

But at this moment a page came into the room with a message from the Queen, and as soon as he received it the King left his seat in the council chamber and went to her.

Alone, among all the people in the castle, the Queen had

realised immediately she awoke from her charmed sleep, exactly what had happened. She remembered the words of the fairy godmother, and she knew that what she had foretold had come to pass, and that the sleep from which she and everybody else in the castle had just awakened had lasted a hundred years.

Her first thought was of her daughter, the Princess Briar-Rose. Where was she, and what had happened to her? If she, too, had merely fallen asleep, all was well, but suppose the doom first spoken by the thirteenth fairy had taken effect?

In a few words she told the King all that was in her mind, and without delay messengers were sent all over the castle to look for the Princess.

In the meantime Briar-Rose and the young Prince were talking together in the ruined tower. For the first time she heard the story of the enchantment, and her eyes grew round with wonder as she listened to her lover's account of the strange things that had happened in the castle. When he told of the great hedge and its cruel thorns, and of the many young men who died in trying to force their way through it, her eyes filled with tears.

"How great their courage was," she sighed. "Oh, if only I could bring them back to life."

But the Prince kissed her tears away, and hastened past that part of his tale, and presently she was smiling again and happy, because she understood that everything had happened as it was bound to happen.

Then the Prince took her hand and raised her from the couch on which she had slept so long, and they went down

the winding stair together and came to the battlements,
where they found a score of breathless people who had been
running up and down in search of her.

And how surprised these people were to find her in that
place, accompanied by a young man they had never seen
before! She seemed to have grown more beautiful than
ever during her long sleep, and they were amazed by her
loveliness.

And how may we describe the joy of the King and Queen when they saw their daughter again and knew that the good fairy had kept her word? The King was so delighted that all he could say was " Bless my soul! bless my soul!" And the Queen could say nothing at all, for she was weeping for joy.

What a feast there was that night! In spite of the hundred years that had gone by it was still the Princess's birthday, and she was in reality no more than fifteen years old, for time had stood still for her. So she had her birthday feast just the same, and it was her betrothal feast too, for the King joined the hands of the young Prince and his daughter and gave them his blessing.

THE END